WALKING IN CHICAGO WITH A SUITCASE IN MY HAND

HALF INCH PRESS

Other books by Matt Morris

Nearing Narcoma
Walking in Chicago with a Suitcase in My Hand
(illustrated edition)
Reckoning Ball
Ordinary Fish/Watt Worris

MATT MORRIS

to Aaron

ACKNOWLEDGMENTS

Many thanks to the following:

ABZ Review: "Here's How," "Metaphysics of Baseball"; *Antietam Review*: "Big Bang"; *Barbaric Yawp*: "Making Valentines," "Sudden Realization of the Perfect Thing to Have Said"; *Blast Furnace*: "As Wordsworth Wandered," "Moon," "White"; *The Blue Bear Review*: "I, the Minotaur"; *Blue Collar Review*: "Blues for Breakfast"; *Blue Mesa Review*: "The Highfalutin Old Coot"; *The Bond Street Review:* "Caveat Emptor," "Poem," "What Do Smart People Think About"; *Caper Literary Journal:* "The Dead Have a Strange Sense"; *DMQ Review*: "Ars Poetica"; *Georgetown Review*: "Blind Spot," "Walking in Chicago with a Suitcase in My Hand"; *The Greater Encyclopedia of Universal Knowledge:* "Imitation of Immortality"; *Great Midwestern Journal*: "Leda & the Sun"; *Hunger Mountain*: "Chimera," "Hole," "Scenes from a Sonata," "Something I'm Thinking About Now"*; Interpoezia:* "Deathwhore," "Erato & Errata," "For Amusement Only," "This Side Up"; *Main Street Rag:* "What's Profoundly Sad"; *Mochila Review*: "As I Lay Dying," "Theory of Fiction"; *New Zoo Poetry Review*: "Part of the Problem"; *Red Booth Review,* "Everything Must Go"; *Rolling Thunder*: "Deathwhore," "For Amusement Only," "On Looking Again at Boswell's Johnson," "Part of the Problem"; *Runes*: "Road Service"*; Segue*: "Idle Days in the Lost City," "Life of God," "Night at the Improv, C. 1600," "Spring Muzzle"; *Swink*: "Washington Crossing the Delaware"*; Timber Creek Review*: "Fish Tale"*; Unlikely Stories:* "New Shoes," "On Looking Again at Boswell's Johnson"

In addition, the following poems appeared in the chapbooks *Here's How*, 2007, Pudding House Publishing and/or *Greatest Hits*, Pudding House Publishing, 2010: "Ars Poetica," "Blues for Breakfast," "Fish Tale," "Here's How," "The Highfalutin Old Coot," "Hole," "Idle Days in the Lost City," "Leda & the Sun," "Life of God," "Metaphysics of Baseball," "Night at the Improv, C. 1600," "Road Service," "Scenes from a Sonata," "Spring Muzzle," and "Theory of Fiction."

Cover art: Matt Morris and M.C. Morris

Walking in Chicago with a Suitcase in My Hand was originally published in late 2015 (despite the copyright date of 2016) as runner-up in the Knut House Press first & possibly only book contest. When Knut House ceased production in 2017, it released its claims on the book & gave all rights back to the author. This edition is a text-only version of the original, which featured Riley A. Vann's photography. It is the way I'd envisioned the book before Knut House asked for illustrations to be published alongside the poems. Although minor changes were made to facilitate formatting issues, aside from correcting spelling & typographical errors, I resisted, for better or worse, the urge to revise, remove, reorder, add, or otherwise alter poems.

Contents

*

*

Bang! Bang! Bang! Bang!

--John Lee Hooker

ROAD SERVICE

Rita's mouth dropped
at the unexpected full-load
pickup pulling off, squealing,
onto the shoulder beside her little
coupe. *Lucky I came by*, Harry (the
name on his shirt) said, sauntering
out of the well-equipped truck. How
could he not, given his profession, notice
her classic chassis in need? Rita tried to take it
all in, mooning over the sight of his bulging
black extended cab 4x4. *Give me a jump?*
She felt around for the latched slot to
pop her hood, which Harry instantly
knew where to find, his thick fingers slip-
ping under her grill. *Oh*, she blurted. One
hand above her head, the other raising the rod
that would prop open her hood, Rita stretched,
leaning over her exposed motor, Harry's breath
on her neck. Jumper cables he kept in his bed snaked
around his arms, he licked his lips. *We'll*, he winked,
get you going. She smiled, sure he knew what went
where & how. His engine throbbing, the jagged teeth
of the cables gently bit the hard nodes of her battery. *Now*,
he yelped. Door swung wide, key in the ignition, left
foot on the ground, her right on the gas, she pumped a bit
wildly, turning over & over until a series of faltering flutters
reached a high-pitched crescendo & shook her car. *How much
do I owe you?* Rita asked, relieved. *Not a damn thing*, Harry shot back.
He gunned his engine. Rita, aglow, gushed even as he sped off, long
after the waggle of his tailgate shrank to just a smudge in her rear view.

Night at the Improv, c.1600

Horrible! retorted Johannes Kepler
to the self-imposed question of how
his mentor, Danish astronomer
Tycho Brahe—whose nose, lost
in a duel, was replaced by a silver
& gold monstrosity—smelled. Goblets
raised, the old guard roared
at Kepler fanning his wry
face for emphasis, feeling
his audience, intelligence thinned
by the Inquisition, might
need a visual aid to
get it. After all, save for a few
snickers, his elliptical orbit
bit flew over their waxed &
wigged heads. Enter Galileo
Galilei onto the stage with vaudevillian
                    aplomb & sly
sight gag revolving around his truly
inspired take on the spyglass,
to wit, his telescope—wink, nudge—
a risibly phallic, ultra outré
gizmo that made the universe,
in its mysterious splendor, little
more than a peep show
for the uptight, meat
pie & mutton crowd, lusting
after a forbidden glimpse
of the celestial
fan dance of Jupiter & her
moons, in details far
above & beyond those accorded
the naked eye. Who or what
could follow an act that exposed
the cosmos, that allowed all

who dared to gape at the infinite
heavenly bodies in motion?
On this night, the pure white light
shone upon a relatively unknown
Dominican friar, Giordano
Bruno, whose regrettable
shtik of what if
a plurality of worlds existed
echoed in dumbness
underscored by fitful howls
of heresy. *Tough crowd,*
quipped Bruno, nervously
mopping his brow, sweating as if
staked to a fire.

A stranger with bad teeth asks for one can
only imagine what. Nobody recognizes
his guttural tongue. Shaking his head, the bar-

keep polishes a tumbler. The stranger babbles
insistently louder. Talk of politics
quiets at a table of locals. Talk

is useless. Tearing his rumpled shirt, the man
bares a map tattooed to his chest, thumps
his fist against a place unknown

miles away. The ceiling fan creaks. A fly
lights on the globe, casting a monstrous
          shadow.

Hole

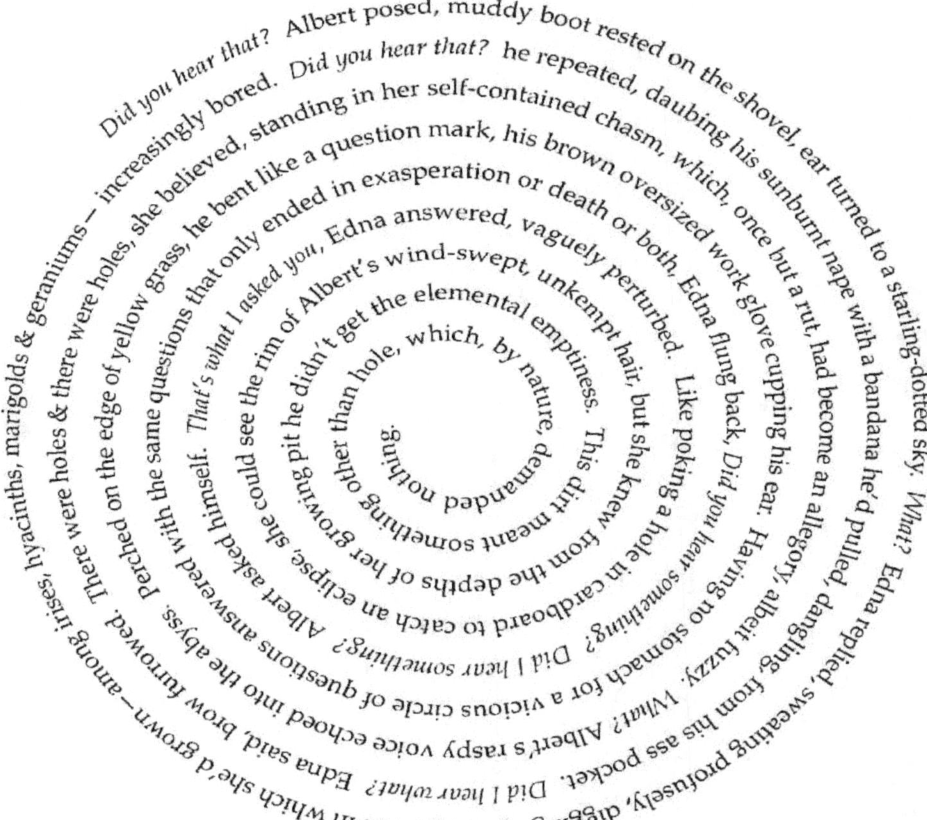

Did you hear that? Albert posed, muddy boot rested on the shovel, ear turned to a starling-dotted sky. *What?* Edna replied, sweating profusely, digging up the garden in which she'd grown —among irises, hyacinths, marigolds & geraniums— increasingly bored. *Did you hear that?* he repeated, daubing his sunburnt nape with a bandana he'd pulled, dangling, from his ass pocket. *Did I hear what?* Edna said, brow furrowed. There were holes & there were holes, she believed, standing in her self-contained chasm, which, once but a rut, had become an allegory, albeit fuzzy. Perched on the edge of yellow grass, he bent like a question mark, his brown oversized work glove cupping his ear. Having no stomach for a vicious circle of questions that only ended in exasperation or death or both, Edna flung back, *Did you hear something? Did I hear something? What?* Albert's raspy voice echoed into the abyss, answered with the same questions Albert asked himself. *That's what I asked you,* Edna answered, vaguely perturbed. Like poking a hole in cardboard to catch an eclipse, she could see the rim of Albert's wind-swept, unkempt hair, but she knew from the depths of her growing pit he didn't get the elemental emptiness. This dirt meant something other than hole, which, by nature, demanded nothing.

LIFE OF GOD

He cried, it rained. He shook
His rattle, thunder echoed
throughout the void. He shat upon
Himself & cherubs flitted about
like flies, zealous to change
His sacrosanct diaper, safety
pins pursed on pious
lips. In school, He made friends
readily—out of popsicle sticks, elbow
macaroni & plenty
of Elmer's. For His science
project—while Buddha fussed
over a Styrofoam
solar system & Vishnu
ate paste—the Almighty showed off
His awe-inspiring, infinite,
fully functional, replete
with flickering lights & soiled humanity,

universe. Lousy
at sports, He counted on angels, rough
& tumble, blackened feathers
flying, to smite the mocking
jocks yoked in the ritual
of pantsing & dragging
His pimply, omnipotent ass
around Heaven's high school track. He aced
the LSATs, raced through
His J.D., resisted
the devilish temptation of politics, opting
instead for a position with Fidelity
Life, where He rose faster
than Jesus, married,
bought a bungalow (mortgaged

beyond redemption) in the burbs, engaged
in extramarital hoo-hahs, divorced,
remarried, begat 2.5
billion children, who, spawned
in His image, disappointed

Him in His dotage. He tossed off sacramental
wine like H_2O, the stubby black
stogie of lost glory clenched
between sin-stained
partials. *Is this
how you want to go?* Mrs. God
ragged over supper, His wizened
face slumped in a cold bowl
of something & sure enough.

Metaphysics of Baseball

Say lefty Don Liddle, shaking off the scandal
of induction, hums the old horsehide
toward the universally held strike
zone of 1954. Baseball, the world
he knows, though given to revolutions,

undergoes less Magnus force than a cross-
seam fastball when hurled "with
the stitches," which, *ipso facto*, will
abruptly descend from its noumenal
plane as if rolling off a table,

resulting in *a priori* routine
grounder (*a posteriori* inning-ending
double-play can be neither
assumed nor ruled out). However, what if
the batter, a Neoplatonist, *i.e.*, Vic Wertz, who,

waiting on a good one, discerns the lack
of backspin, adjusts his stride & weight
shift early in his swing, its slight
uppercut well-timed & directed to
hit the pitch squarely, sending it

screaming toward an ontological
argument? How far it goes
depends upon such variables as space, time, whether
the ball is smooth, scuffed, or necessarily
exists, all of which Willie Mays, back

turned, glove outstretched, intuits, Q.E.D. Chasing
the drive deep into the epistemological
gap at the Polo
Grounds, he spins & throws
simultaneously without regard

to paradox, the catch, *das ding-an-sich*,
indicative of positivism, treating
any discourse anent the nature
of reality as academic, ergo unworthy
of the discussion devoted hereinbefore.

WALKING IN CHICAGO WITH A SUITCASE IN MY HAND

Howlin' Wolf's growling, slouched
over a bluesy guitar on the corner,
hammering & stretching strings, bending

notes & somehow rhyming the title line with his
succinct explanation–twenty
words, tops–that the woman he still

loves, as evidenced by his pained rendition, told him
to leave because, he laments, he loves drinking, playing
the ponies & laying out all hours. But that's

not who I am–the guy in faded jeans & brown
bomber jacket, blue shirttail hanging out, glasses
smudged, hair clinging to my face, trying to

remember what the doorman said: *Left
on Lake to catch the L?* Trudging down Stetson,
I've lived inside my head long enough to know

my way around, but not Chicago, rain
falling with the temperature. Here on pleasure
for the weekend, it's (literally,

figuratively & on every level, both Upper
& Lower Wacker) over–& over
the jagged teeth of discordant architecture

the sad refrain plays as Howlin's blowing
his harp–a train rumbling ever
faster, then fading–not merely tapping, but stamping

his leather sole against the wet
pavement. In the song, the suitcase
symbolizes burden & as mine grows

heavy, I switch hands. Rain turns
to snow. At the station, I realize how little I know
about the woman, but it scarcely

matters how pretty she is & smart, if she speaks
with a slight accent, whether her sweater's
stylish with soft contours. To understand

the blues, the singer seems to suggest, you need
only know somewhere in this city lives
someone who'll–he mutters almost

indecipherably–be happy when I'm gone.

I myself figured out that peculiar form of mathematics and
harmonics that was strange to all the world but me.

—Jelly Roll Morton

HERE'S HOW

To determine the area of the soul, you
must first convert the imaginary

into a real number equal to the sum
of your life experiences. You may need

a calculator to extrapolate your childhood
on the farm, dreaming in the corn-

field of purity & right, as an integer greater
or less than zero. Let x represent

the lance corporal on the red-eye who
became the coefficient of your grief. Remember

to subtract your lost faith before
factoring the depth of your Being.

You'll discover love & death are natural
logarithms. Multiply to proceed.

Night School

Norman forgot his math
book because when he
went to kiss his wife
goodbye, he found in-
stead a blue Post-it
Note that said something
he didn't like or
understand, walked out,
angry, unlucky,
& unloved, then had
to share, gazing up
at the dirty black-
board sky, a book with
a flatulent man
munching gingersnaps.

Each cracked, faded floor
square represented
that awkward moment
in which bifocals
flew off Norman's nose
when he'd violently
achooed, the distri-
butive property
proven, Q.E.D.
But even without
his glasses, Norman
saw himself clearly
as the product of
cheap irony, the
going rate, feeling
around random legs
& spaces until
the inattentive
heel of a loafer

crushed the back of his
hand.
      Precisely what—
asked the professor,
propping the window
open with a large
abacus—*is the
hypotenuse of
an isosceles
triangle opposed
to a lost sense of
self-worth, uh, Norman?*

Mad wind whooshed papers
throughout the classroom,
as a voice that no
one recognized, not
even Norman, whose
own thoughts meandered,
answered with sputtering
uncertainty, thus:

*a) the path to truth;
b) nothing outside its linguistic form;
c) not actual, the ultimate value cannot be known;
d) anxiety, guilt, desire;
e) 7½, same as my hat.*

of humor. Given the punch line, they never, even if it tickles,
laugh, their funny bones fully exposed like the rest
of their skeletal remains. Puns fall on deaf ears, so don't
ask with elbow & wink if the late gentleman's "ghoul-friend"
is good in the sack or better in sackcloth. Boneheaded,
he'll stare blankly at you as if just informed of his demise. Props, how-
ever absurd, aren't bona fide knee-slappers, slapstick misses
the mark & clever tricks can't bring an audience
back. Limericks? Hell

                  no. Riddles? The dead won't
hazard a guess. Decomposition doesn't allow
much ribbing, however gentle. Dust finds nothing amusing
about ethnic shtik. Political jabs lack
relevance; conceptual humor–it's your funeral. How about
dolling up for the wake like J. Edgar on a blind
date, blonde wig & way

        too much makeup? Expect deadpan
expressions in lieu of guffaws, no matter
how far "out there" you go. They're already there, not
breathing in the graveyard's long black grass, crickets chirping, wind
whisking a few dried leaves past
rows of headstones, reminding you of one certainty–dying's
rolling off a log. It's comedy

that's a bitch.

CHIMERA

I'm sleeping with my hand
between the cream
pages of Louise Glück's
Descending Figure, Mom's ghost
banging on the other side
of the door, telling me to get up,
umbilical cord knotted
at either end to an empty soup can, her
rasp resonating across the murky
void of whatever is & isn't
dream, where I'm falling

through the inverted bowl of sky
dumping its soggy flakes
on a red rooftop two blocks
from the tracks. Whenever
a train passes, it shakes
the faded cowboy sheets wound
around me, a comic
mummy, shamefully hugging
a stuffed dog. G.I. Joe, Creepy Crawlers,
spare bike parts & the like litter
the floor. A model sits on my chest

of drawers–a funny car dragster, Ed
"Big Daddy" Roth's Rat Fink,
the rotund rodent's candy apple
tongue extended, metallic blue claw
clutching the oversized stick's
eight ball. I don't understand
exactly how I wound up here,
but I'm quick to give up
donkey's years of memories,
so nobody screamed
naked on the lawn, nobody

scared the tits off the neighbors'

yak topiary & nobody died. Mom carries
on like I'm late for the big test. Once
out of bed, I can't go back. I want
nothing more than plastic soldiers
with missing extremities to stand up
& plead for sleep. But my mouth won't
work & the dead don't listen.

POEM

Beginning as a series of line
shifts, a mix of illogic
& machines, of geometric
forms & geographic formations,

each exploited by the rich
possibilities of the unspoiled
canvas, it moves through air-
less architecture. Stripped

of abstraction, it turns
animal, violent–
its frenzy tamed, harnessed,
caged. How tempting

to extend a hand to caress,
to squeeze the soft,
full, black-as-fruit skin
of the thin & vulnerable,

the nearly human
figure, outlined in red
smudges, squirming inside. Nose
bowed, eyes closed, it grows

smaller until, slipping through
the bars, a delicate winged
creature takes flight, whistling
an inimitable song.

IDLE DAYS IN THE LOST CITY

You can't ignore the contented smile
that graces each one of the upwards
of thirty participants, faces tilted
toward the sun. Caught on the breeze, their
constructions lift
            in a dazzling array. Those
of you who've made one
already know it takes more than wind
for such a show, requiring
hours, even days, of preparation. Watching
J.C. cutting balsa, do you
know what he wants?

                Judging from the length
& number of strips at his feet, you
may guess he's making a box,
but surprisingly, he's building
a gigantic ring, which, once
covered in gold foil, he'll let fly
his lofty design
                to ask for Lucie's
fetching hand. Meanwhile, crosstown,
Lucie, wheels
turning, drums her nubby
pencil eraser lightly on the drawing
desk. What's reflected
in her wire frame lenses
aren't postage stamps,
but blueprints for a large-

            scale dragon. But just
past the foreboding
wings, penciled in meters, do you see
over her shoulder the likeness
of a man in the doorway? He walks
toward her, she removes

her glasses. In the dark, you
hear J.C.'s distant tapping,
         echoing his heart.
You shake your head
at the crystal ball,
but maybe as that gold
ring soars overhead, Lucie
offers a plausible, perfectly
innocent explanation. Or maybe
J.C.'s foil-wrapped dream
falters & falls, the fault
lying with schematics, not
with Lucie.
         Or maybe
something unforeseen
overshadows the lives of a few
who look to the heavens
for answers. The truth
of the matter–well, you probably
already know.

Screwing in the sky! The lucky
couple, lifted
from R.
Crumb comics, hover
near a peak, purple
nimbus ringing
the snow-capped

knob while a slumped
seraph puffs
a fatty, peering
through holy robes
in heaven's closet, the door
uncannily ajar,
chalky wing tips
jutting through
the cheek
of Stuart's unfinished
portrait of

dolorous George. Thunder
& the Almighty
drops in, & if a lightning
bolt's any clue,
Mr. Big isn't
pleased. Who
is? Not
George, his cloudy likeness
darkening around the feathery
gash. Not the angel
snuffing
out his smoldering butt. Not
the twosome dissipating
like scuds

in *cumulus interruptus*.

27

                                    O

lordy, honey, but I miss your

                               sweet dough-

    iness, farther

        than any cloud

            from me.

Leda & the Sun

A lemon wedge pushing through ice cubes,
which are actually clouds, the sun beats down
on the woman. As if feeding a flame, she
re-lubes the backs of her thighs, her ass
round as a turtle shell. Knowing the sun
isn't really a fruit, she shakes the sand
from her peroxidic mop. Fingers climb
her back to find the vague string that loosens

with a quick tug her small swimsuit & she
wriggles free. Now the sun's on her however
she turns, her skin tingling with each ray's
penetration. Being so undone, does
she shudder in light of the changing tide
when the indifferent sun goes down on her?

If the whole of my life occurred
                         in one day, I'd walk in just
             about now, glasses
                         fogged, skyline
           of denim sprawling in the ubiquitous
        butt cleavage over Naugahyde
                         stools. Beers
bloodied with tomato
                                   juice to wash away
                 sundry sins & salty
                         nuts spilled over frosted
                 mugs, cracked
floor shiny, sticky
                         as memory of dark
           sex in a drunken
                         booth, blurry hair band
on the jukebox fading. I remember—
                 my hands remember
           you, the pinball
         machine I'd lit up, turned
over, dial rotating
                         in a display of multiple
             O's above the bikini beauties like
                         balloons
       in a comic strip. Hand
                 jammed in my pants, I feel
           for a quarter, slide it
                         in that wondrous
           slot, fingering the magic
button. The Reds pasting
                         the Dodgers on the wall-
             mounted portable, Fanny taps another
                         draft, slides a big-
head toward someone, maybe

Dad, thirty years lighter, laughing too
hard. You moan a throaty
ooh as my ball zips up

the chute & down
the playdeck, caroming bumper
to bumper, bells
dinging, lights
flashing. I lean
into the casing, thrusting my
pelvis just so
to nudge the shiny
marble for big
points toward the target
between the V of your
outstretched legs, slap
the flipper, flick the ball back
to ricochet off the top
wildly, prompting random
bonuses. Dad in a sweaty
wife-beater, draped
across the wobbly pool
table for an improbable
shot, misses, leaving his dumpy
girlfriend–halter
top, hot pants & all–an easy
setup. Leaning over, lining
up the shot, she squeals,
farting as he gooses her
with a cue. I nearly
jump when she shrieks. Your
special lit, I've become
the ball, banging
toward the hole, determined
to shoot to the top of your
high scores tally, my
initials tattooed there so the next
guy who plays you knows

30

what I know. Tilt
of earth brings summer,
    & fans–perched
in windows, dangling
   from rafters, oscillating
behind the bar–blow dirty
    streamers. Dad swipes
his stubbled chin hard with
    his sleeve & howls
in the boozy chorus.

31

*If you got something you don't want other people to know,
keep it in your pocket.*

–Muddy Waters

BLIND SPOT

Listening to nothing,
wishing he were drinking it

instead of this bitter
coffee spilled
from the moon's

empty, upside down
Styrofoam cup
he's driving into, the old
me, blinded

in one eye by the bb
of the working poor, the chromo-
somal drunken
rage at his lousy life, not to
mention soon-to-be ex-

wife, tired
of job, bills, bill
collectors, dogs always
barking, he races
the wisp of road to the foot
of the hill, doesn't find me in his

mirrors, doesn't glimpse
a future or the impending now
hauling ass, but
barreling down on him
at light speed, it's
my new & improved
self, swerving & laying

on the horn. I cut
the wheel sharply & pump

bad brakes, spinning out
across the dark
median, the blank
slate of my invisible
history fast-forwarding
into oncoming traffic, smack-

ing guardrail's unexpected
soft hand. Stopping
dead, I roll
down my window, wave
I'm OK, even though I know
he can't see his future
incarnation, still shaking
the tight ball
of his fist.

FISH TALE

A line rises from the sun-
streaked surface. A bird

twitters in willows slouched
along the shore. Out

on the river, the angler
sleeps. His dream

catch, pondering the lure, abruptly
bites & runs. Such

strength, speed–the small
boat keels, & the angler

shatters the liquid
mirror. Dragged head-

first, he body surfs, blue miles
becoming ocean. Letting go

his rod, plummeting through murky
depths of the sub-

conscious, past the suppressed
shrimp of a kid–swallowed up

& spit out by a cruel,
anonymous school–who never

took a mate, suddenly
swimming in women, he fills
                    his aching

lungs as he breaststrokes
over ripples of flesh, crests

of nipples kissing either
cheek, no matter where

or how he turns.
          When the angler
wakes, slapping a mosquito,

sun burnt, pole dangling
in the calm, he rubs

his chin, reels in, recasts
his line. Deep down,

he believes, still & all, lies
the big sucker.

Moon

I'd gone to the river for water, but trudging
back to the cabin, I found the unmistakable silver
sliver of the quarter Moon in my bucket. No wonder
the sky had clouded: I'd accidentally scooped

the Moon up instead. Not virtue
alone stopped me from keeping it. Unlike
the monied snobility who want, say, the *Mona
Lisa* to hang in their loo, I lacked

the space, so I turned around, sloshing cold
water over the sides of the pail, slogging down the slope
to the riverbank to put the Moon back
where I'd found it. When I got there, wouldn't you

know, I discovered the Moon had seeped
out what seemed, in retrospect, a rather conspicuous
hole in my bucket. I retraced my steps, scoured
the wooded path, the thousand

eyes of the dark looking too, but uncovered
nary a clue of the Moon or its dissipated ooze. Soon
dawn came like a barge on the river, the workaday
world of light in its hold. Over the next few nights, I took

Barkley out to pick up the trail, though this proved
fruitless, save for a few wild
berry vines stumbled upon, thorns & all. O
I was set to quit when he practically dragged me by

the leash to a smallish cemetery up a hill. I felt
queasy passing through the rickety
gate, but gazing upward, I caught the glimmer
of the Moon, beaming down at me from atop

a tall pine. *How did you get up there?* I asked
like a coyote howling. Not really expecting a reply,
I nevertheless heard a dry lecture on the science behind
condensation, plus a few condescending comments

concerning the phases of the Moon. Letting Barkley run
free, I marveled at his vaulting, nearly
somersaulting, with the aplomb of a circus
pony over headstones & romping crazily–like

a lark flitting from larch to larch–across sunken
plots until, in the time it takes to suck a lemon
drop to a nub, he'd disappeared. *Barkley!*
I called & whistled, begging pardon of the Moon, which

now was nowhere to be seen either.
Out of the blackness, Barkley,
big floppy ears flapping, came bounding
toward me as if after a rabbit or chased

by a rabbit's ghost. His paws, muddy
from digging, caught me so off-guard, I fell
backward into an open grave, where, the breath
knocked out of me, I saw, clenched

gingerly between his teeth, what I took
at first to be a human skull, though damned
if, upon further reflection,
it wasn't the Moon.

The Distant Sea

Stars gone, God dead, the unknown
vessel drifted, hopelessly lost. Pounding
surf tossed her across deserted
waters, turning windward toward
disaster. Splintered hull bobbing, all
at once plunging, refusing
to come back up, she spewed drunk
& dreaming men, sprawled
in their cabins, into chaos & further
oblivion. No panic, no flailing arms.
Head tilted toward the swirling
surface light, the old
sailor tried to call out: nothing
save an involuntary gasp. Eyes
empty as they closed.
    Was he asleep?
He wanted to roll onto his back
to wake up but descended
paralyzed into black, as if the sun
itself, unhooked from its golden
chain, sank extinguished
below. No up, no down, yet he kept
going–motion is actual–his ribs
cracked, his lungs collapsed
in the depth's frigid embrace, unaware
of the other existence, the beast
feeding in the darkness, devouring,
like a squid,

him. He lived inside
the whale's belly, Spartan quarters
furnished via a catalog
of shipwrecks: the tragedy
of the *Viscount* providing

an antique glass-
enclosed bookcase, among
its hold *Moby Dick* (moderate
wear due to rubbing, some
tears)*, Three Men
in a Boat* (binding shows
minimal use) & *The Rime
of the Ancient Mariner* (dust
jacket missing, slight
damage to spine); the doomed
Essex bequeathing a braided
rug embossed with a 19th
century schooner; the harpoon, displayed
with irony on the abdominal wall,
gobbled up easy as lime
sea foam when the *Lorelei* went down,
taking a hundred good men
with her.
   One day a pine
box washed up with a crow as big
as a man inside–a portent
of death, the old salt thought, but as it turned
out, the bird proved an entertaining
conversationalist, well-versed
in philosophy & politics, as well
as a skilled chess tactician who'd
play hour upon hour losing
nary a piece, bishop &
knight breaking, ever
& again, the gray-haired sea-
dog's flank. In matching wing
chairs, they sat long
into the evening, asea
in complex stratagems. Ticklish,
the leviathan snorted when
the crow plucked a long, elegant

quill for the old gob, who, lighting
a meerschaum recovered
from the *Lusitania*, jotted
down his wry observations.
For instance: *Whale-ness
equals wholeness.* Or: *It always smells
of fish around here, but on the bright
side, we never run out of oil.*

On Looking Again at Boswell's Johnson

"It is much easier," a sweaty Johnson
reckons, slipping into ladies' pink
merino drawers, "not to write like a man
than to write like a woman."
Which is true

if you write with your cock. Easier still—
as we observe Boswell, silk slipper alighted
for leverage on the master's rump
pad, tugging corset laces
tight for the honor-

able, honorary doctor, who, expelling
wind like a whale, adjusts
his ponderous falsies—is not to write
at all. Period. End of sentence.
Ah! but these things—

as casting a critical eye at the critic, batting
his lashes spastically & applying
a coquettish mole upon
a rouged & powdered cheek, suggests—
are not as simple

as they seem. For one often feels certain
inborn urges to dip the quixotic
quill, so to speak. The doctor advises those
with such desires to go about it early
of a morning, with the crusty

moon's elegantly plumed tricorn
just going down, then "crowd to the public
rooms at night," for "real

delight" comes–if you know your Johnson–not
from wit alone, but a hale

& hearty fuck. Of course, one can do it
any time, Johnson clucks, "if he will
set himself *doggedly* to it." Winking, he whistles "Air
on the G-String" whilst conjuring Sapphic
couplets, triplets & all

forms of sextilla to encourage
budding authors. Never shy, his phony
coiffure piled high with pomade & flour
a bit like Mme. Pompadour, hoop
skirt hoisted to flaunt

petticoats & garters, he provocatively
gestures to "every young man . . . to do it as fast
as he can" &–according to Boswell
behind his ornate spread fan–
"to start promptly."

THEORY OF FICTION

As the balding keynote speaker's
topic continues to thin
the conference room out
of which she'd ducked, Rosie
steps into the bizarre
contraption that had come
at last, a unique tram,
according to the brochure,
that would travel via pulleys &
cables six hundred odd feet
up the architectural
marvel of the Gateway Arch.
        Prof. Freitag, nose deep
in a dog-eared Lawrence, growls
& grovels, squeezing in, pawing
Rosie's knee ostensibly
for balance as he sits. Face to
face, the space between them
alternately a vase for Rosie
to place her thoughts—her thorny
affair having withered
inevitably into depression, stem-
ming from episodes of hit-
        &-run fucking—her dewy
gaze drops like petals into
her hands, cupped in the lap
of her modest floral-print
sundress. The herky-jerky
car rattles, lurches, climbs,
clunks, squelches, then–popping
like the worn balloon
of a pipedream–everything,
save the perspiration streaming
down her purfled neckline, stops

several hundred feet above a number
of picnickers footnoting the Jefferson
National Expansion Memorial
grounds.

       Something snaps. The tram
shakes, & the specter of
death, Prof. Freitag muses, perhaps
had unbeknownst wrangled
a last-minute ride. Rosie
smiles wryly, unclasping
her frilly wisp of a frock, breasts
toppling out of lacy red
cups lifted from Victoria's
Secret. The pro-
fessor, with a meretricious
       slurp, licks
his fingertip, sighs
& flips the sticky
page, firm in his
conviction this
is part of the fiction
forged in the virtual
furnace of the tram, owing
to fear & lack
of ventilation, but
even in denial, the petals
of Rosie's garb, spilling off
her shoulders, swirl
around the crucial
point
       of her thighs. The dirty
human cage, creaking
above the renewed
racket of gears, slowly
engages, the tension

of cables straining against
opposing forces–whether
temporary mechanical
failure or hard-to-
fathom, backbreaking,
impossible love–as it ascends, if
the old model holds, the shiny
slope, its plot
of characters born in each car, disparate
souls thrown together
by lot, reaching
the anticipated, compelling
& for some, life-
          altering peak. When
the door squeaks
open to denouement, Prof.
Freitag grunts he needs
to shit while Rosie,
nipples jutting, strolls by the well-
lubricated Legionnaires & plaid
families, gawking outcasts all
converging upon the observation
windows & wonders
in the panorama of East
St. Louis if anyone, even
hypothetically, has ever succumbed
& jumped.

BIG BANG

Later, the earliest man
& woman lay by the muddied
puddles of their prehistoric
sweat, now oceans, & blew
clouds into the ancient flicker

of unfolding skies. These shadows,
lumped together, making fiery
mountains of primordial
friction, gave unimaginable
creatures no longer

in existence names nobody
recollects, except for distant
relatives, mostly on my father's
side. *E.g.*, great-
great *ad absurdum* Aunt

Luzdivina, cantankerous, corn
pipe centenarian, & her setaceous
daughters, Fedelma & Paudeen.
Or any of my toothy,
knuckle-walking cousins

christened Flem. Or poor
Uncle Annis, salesman
of sorts–the sort only lonely
housewives required–who
thought the odd glimmer

across the room he'd staggered
home to that long ago night
was an incidental slice
of moon before he heard the big
bang.

LIKE FRANÇOIS VILLON

You shove the pistol in the store clerk's horse
face & demand the contents of the drawer.
Scared shitless, he does what you say, of course.
It strikes you funny, the old saw "over

a barrel," re: the glint of your semi-
automatic Glock. Maybe you'll use it
as part of some intricate simile–
the pun, you chuckle, not the gun. Such wit-

ticisms of yours would be lost if you'd
become distracted writing lines. *Quickly!*
you bark in anger. Tone–like rent, clothes, food,
but most of all verse–matters. Robert Bly,

you bang the counter, said you had talent
at a seminar for writers in Vermont.

PART OF THE PROBLEM

1

Koo, some cunt my brother used to fuck, calls
looking for him. *He moved*, I grunt into the phone. *Jesus,
over four months ago.* The digital
clock-radio red light flashes into focus. *You
know what time it is? Sorry,* she says in that tight,
squeaky voice girls adopt when they know they're
a pain in the ass but want you to remember they've
got tits. *Forget it*, I tell her, then ask if she'd

like Chaz's new number because I'm sure he needs
a midnight wake-up call too. She sniffs. I'm not positive
if she's just being snooty or ready to cry. But she's not
a total skank, so to keep her from blubbering, I ask,
What's up–all she needs to launch into what a model
prick my brother is, never returning her messages

2

& not listening. *Fucking-A*, I say, ogling oily,
muff-diving lezbos in *Penthouse*. It's the last days
of '79 & I'm a short curly from blowing
peter snot in my briefs when she wants to know if
I'd mind if she came over, she says, to see
if my asshole brother left her *Let It Be* LP.
You know where I am, I tell her, cool as–hell,
I don't know, Barry White. Sacks

of garbage pile on top of each other in a fuckfest
of reek, stacks of dishes rise out of the sink higher than
spires off a Zeppelin jacket & mice stomp around like fairies
in boots. Goddam, I feel lucky. I don't clear the sofa–
if she wants to sit, there's the bed, which isn't
exactly tidy either, but serves the greater purpose,

3

despite some stains. I gargle & brush in case
Dr. Tongue is called upon to perform
his magic, even slap on some cheap-ass
cologne. Flexing my pecs in the mirror, I hear
the bell, throw on a shirt without bothering to
button it. *Holy shit*, I blurt at the door, forgetting
my radical come-on line because I notice Koo's totally
knocked up. Her eyes look really red & she says, all

agitated, *You going to let me in or what?* Like Princess
Leia, hair balled over her ears, nose up & out of joint, she tramps
past me, snapping, *This place stinks. Hey, you're the one
moaning about your Beatles record*, I remind her. OK, she's
pregnant & that sucks, but how's that my problem? It's not
like I'm the fucking Ayatollah holding her shit hostage. What

4

a bitch. All I recall Chaz leaving was an empty Johnny
Walker Red behind the radiator, a turd bobbing
in the toilet & a wadded notice from the clinic that he'd caught
the clap. *Go fucking nuts*, I say, showing her back
to my bedroom, where my albums wrapped around
the baseboard. *Omigod*, she hoots, eyes
big & blue as my balls. I got over
a thousand records–no shit–& if she wants

to rifle them, what the hell. She slips
out of her rat fur collar coat, folds
it into a pillow & slowly lowering, plops
her twat down sidesaddle, denim skirt riding
up to her crack. I got a boner deluxe. *Ooh*, she gasps,
pulling *It's a Beautiful Day* out. *I love this*. I don't

5

know about love, but I'm goddamned she even heard of
the band. I guess if you slut around enough, you get a taste
of everything. *Put it on*, she begs. *I only listen to shit*

that fucked up when I'm high, I tell her, my way
of politely saying get bent, but pawing around
in her purse, she fishes out a warped little joint,
so I park my butt, flip my Bic & thumb
through the covers with her. Funny, we both like the Stones,

the Ramones, Devo & Costello better than that fat fuck
Presley, who sucks even from the grave. She likes Bowie,
but he's a drag queen, I point out, giggling
way too long about that. Maybe
it's the reefer, but I'm turned on, especially
with her whining about her boobs being swollen, as if

      6
they've taken on dimensions reserved for a sci-fi
skin flick about the mutating radioactive
fallout from Three Mile Island. *They're so
sensitive*, she pouts, gently
massaging them. My cock's good as
poking through my pants. It's going
to be hell getting up for work, but I'll probably
call in with the shits, so I ask if she wants

a brew. Down to the roach, she feeds me pure-D
bullshit about alcohol being bad for the baby. *You don't
mind if I swill one*? I ask like I give a fuck. All of a sudden,
she wells up blubbering how Russia, for no good
reason, invaded some third-world shithole, how
history is a record of military conquest

      7
& might, how much she hates that what's inside her
is simply cannon fodder. *You dumbass*, I console her. *The U.S.
is too pussified to nuke those camel-fuckers in Tehran, much
less do anything about the cocksucking commies*. I need that beer
in the worst way but can't stop gawking at her, dark
blue sweater lifted, lightly stroking her bare

belly. It's none of my business, but I ask anyway, *Who
is the father?* She shuts her eyes, whispers, *God*

knows. I figure Chaz, but she doesn't want me
to tell him–Christ, she's a whore. Besides, the world's all sorts
of crazy shit nobody knows dick about. Like before tonight,
I never knew you could fuck someone with a bun
in the oven, which you can, but you've got to do it extra
slow–& brother, there's nothing wrong with that.

God, I'm just a fat bald guy, 60 years old, singing the blues, you know?

—Joe Cocker

Scenes from a Sonata

Exposition

As a child I thought slips
hanging on my closet door
were angels. Now I see
the surly face of god
staring down from the ceiling. You
were fat & crushed me, then
had the nerve to ask if I'd
ever made love to a man
before. Implying what?
I was the closest
thing to a virgin you—a moral
pygmy—would have.

Development

I remember your thumbing
pages of Michelangelo
the morning I came
to apologize, barreling
my Kawasaki over
your gladiolas. You hated me,
but what made you think
I would stroke the hair
of the dog that early? I
am always spiteful.

Recapitulation

You thought yourself clever—as if
you could trick me with your
lure of a quickie! The next
time I saw you, you'd grown
whiskers & slicked your inky
curls back with Crisco, though
your swishy corduroys
made me laugh.

Coda

If only you knew how I've
sulked & skulked, pants
around my ankles, scratching
at your window! I confess
I made a crapper out
of a birdbath, but only so
much can be said before 6 a.m.
sans phone calls &
police. O! lift
the latch that I may serenade
you with my snazzy concertina.

BLUES FOR BREAKFAST

Eggs glared sunny-side
up at him when he'd ordered
scrambled. Biscuits
burnt, potatoes neither
hashed nor browned, he spit
coffee, shouting across
the checkerboard
diner, *How about shaking that
jelly over here, honey!* Wadded
hose crawling down her
varicose knees, she couldn't
waddle fast enough to thwart
his whistling with one hand, banging
a spoon against his empty
mug with his other. *You got
a problem,* she drawled,
thick lip arched like fat
Elvis in drag, *tell it
to your mama.*

                    Where,
he barked, arrowy
eyebrows accentuating
yellowy goo dribbling
off his brandished fork,
*are my goddam
grits?* Her curled lip
quivered while a salty
globule sneaked
down her cheek, spilling
her life's minutiae: piss-
stained sofa, TV on
the fritz, unemployed,
unwed daughter knocked
up again, the father, unlike

58

the future, unknown
or in jail, everything–down
to her flea-infested
mutt run over that a.m.–
rising in her gorge.

Fork dropping
onto his plate, he
flashed a crooked
smile of contrition, knowing
unspoken hardships
of quarterly sales
red-lining, wife
screwing the hard-
boiled, good old boy sheriff, dis-
obedient, maladjusted
kids keen on self-mutilation
& rap. His voice gone
soft & gravelly, he offered
a stick of Wrigley's
with his apology. *Gum,*
she sniffed, lifting
her lacy aproned skirt to grab
her crotch,
this.

when they lift dry eyes above
      foggy bifocals, resting low
upon noble noses & note,
      before thumbing another page of
The Great Encyclopedia of
      Universal Knowledge, the flower–sepal,
stamen, pistil, *et al.*, diagramed
      & labeled–swaying outside, out
of context? Are artists, given
      the same perspective, drawn
to gouaches à la Dufy, a quasi
      erotic O'Keeffe pastel, or *The Tomb*
of the Wrestlers by Magritte? Or porn
      stars–do they loll naked under
a sunlamp, spreading lush lobelia
      lips for the camera, wet petals
shimmering in the scintillating syn-
      thetic breeze? O the whinny
of the packhorse unloaded
      of its burden, the old saw
goes, but what about
      my sorry ass? 3 a.m. & I
stare at the Rorschach rain-
      stained ceiling, the flower in its
dark blue vase fragrantly fore-
      shadowing love, death, whatever. How,
if asked, would the flower respond?
      Why, one offers, speaking
on behalf of the bouquet, *we're*
      merely jonquils.

I, THE MINOTAUR,

get the myth thing, but I don't see my kine
self as some sort of metaphor for "man's
suppressed animalistic urges" (Fein-
berg 110).
     Do sacrificial virgins,
tearing up & down the maze untouched by
the optimistic sun, think of themselves
as symbols of, what,
      lost youth? Then why should I
consider my cretin hooves an old wives'
tale? Are these monstrous horns of my father
merely figures of speech? The cock & bull
story of my strange conception, rather
than literary,
     conveys literal
truth,
   which you'd know if you knew anything
of my mother's frustration with the king.

1) Return of Geppetto

Girly thingies, red & lacy, dangle
from the bedpost & puddle the parquet
floor of what used to be the dead man's
workshop. From his ethereal

cloud, he swoops down, dismayed
to find his wooden-head, fathered
from the purity of the old toy maker's
heart, squandering his dream made real

life on carnality. Pinocchio, smug,
smudged grin paling, lies entangled
with a pair of marionettes, their silky
strings like strands of angel hair.

2) Back to Emporia

No more Scarecrow. He drew
the short straw, crucified

in the cornfield. Tin Man,
broken like a rusty nail, fell

into obsolescence & despair. Poor
Lion, teeth extracted

for souvenirs, roared
his last, too feeble

to care. Toto, Glinda,
the Wizard gone, the family

farm supplanted by a mall,
Dorothy shambled down

the double yellow line
of the blacktop, her rag doll

dress flapping in the wind
of an eighteen wheeler,

muttering, *We're not
in the Emerald*

City anymore, to the pretend
hen clutched to her breast.

Making Valentines

Widow Mrs. Carey, no kids outside
her daycare, set her toy
poodle, dyed purple to match

her bouffant, down on purple
linoleum, framed by
purple walls, door

& ceiling. Creasing red
construction paper, she snipped
along the penciled

outline of what resembled a comic
drunk's bulbous nose, showing how to cut
a heart out to give to someone

special. Lauren shaped a perfect
heart, announcing, red cheeked, her
marriage, date not set, to her

high school sweetheart, fated to meet
scant weeks before her junior prom.
Gerald cut opposite the fold, stupidly

rendering his heart into big tear-
shaped halves portending messy
divorce, alcoholism & suicide. Amy

trimmed the top pointy
as the bottom so, unfolded, it sprouted
horns that bespoke

temptations of illicit, sometimes
dangerous sex, while Danny—who
could figure his square

cut-out meant he'd
disappear onto a milk carton? Left
arm in a cast, broken

for the second
time in three months, I maneuvered safety
scissors with my unnatural

right like hedge clippers, zigzagging
along the sloppy
curved line. Pissed I'd used

the last of the red, Mrs. Carey, poodle
yipping, slapped a blue
sheet in front of me for my ragged

little heart, which, she
warned, no mat-
ter what, I'd just have to live with.

I'm heading
to work when
Missy, my ex, stops
by to borrow my
yellow-for-shit
Chevette. Alive, she
hated the thing, so
it's odd that
after "the accident"
she wants it, but
              I hand
her the keys. Late per
usual for my shift, I
don't see her
again until dark. I'm
shlepping a crate of
dried, diced, assorted
animal parts across
the lot to the service
door when she pops out
of nowhere. I nearly
let Chef's secret
recipe slip when I remember
my car, flipped in
my mind on its
back, one squeaky
wheel spinning. Missy
lowers her gaze.
I feel a stirring inside
the crate coming
back to life & damn if
it doesn't plop splat
at my feet. I'm ankle-
deep in miscellaneous

meat spillage. *You're
funny*, Missy
drawls, her eyes matter-
of-fact, *& I don't
mean in a good way.*

Spring Muzzle

Turnbridge Wells, 1820

If it were something I said
I didn't do–Ludlow began, sotto voce,
breeze dying in the bedroom window, burgundy
drapes drawn aside, overlooking the garden.

Clara, feigning interest in her most
improving book, never allowed
her bright round eyes
to lift. *Doesn't signify*, she sniffed, adopting

a tone usually reserved for her Yorkshire
pup. She understood too well the ordeal
he'd suffered–& at his age! Sighing, Clara
absently turned the page to the ball-

room of her past, her apricot
mull with lace overskirt & van dyke hem bespeaking
her provincial tastes as she indulged in pleasant
flirtations, an angel dancing on

a pinhead. Ludlow's
cravat, tied rashly in the mathematical–
as usual, in want of review–appeared
for all the world a Gordian knot

whenever he tried to speak
the stuff & nonsense of his heart, but
as he belonged to the gentry, she–
one & twenty when the banns

were read–belonged to him. Sweeping
over the discontent of years in which

he'd, at length, made clear her wifely duties, past
leaves torn from a ledger, meant to

mask the wretched pounds he'd
trifled away at his club on whist, port
& tawdry bits of skirt, Clara reflected
upon the wet cobblestone of a fortnight ago

when, with wool coat's claw-hammered
tails violently flapping, a "princely" figure
wove his velocipede willy-nilly through
the promenade, dinging a tinny

bell & caroming off an orphan's
flower cart into a waiting
phaeton, a flurry of mixed bouquets
spilling by Ludlow's bloody frame. He stared

blankly up, calling, now as then, his dear,
sweet Clara. Her stalk of patience
having long since snapped, she loathly
set her four-edged book aside, smiled

less than charitably & smoothed his clump
of linens. The afternoon felt
somewhat aphrodisiacal–Clara held
in willful disregard Ludlow's goose

feather pillow over his muffled cries–what
with grosbeaks pecking ripe
sunflowers & bees
buzzing the bee balm.

WHITE

pines moan, buckled
with ice & grief. Dogs, hungry,
in a snarl after Karuka

disappeared, slog through end-
less snow that scumbles field
& firmament. No sky

means no god. What remains
dangles from creaking
branches. One snaps, collapses,

frightening the skittish
team. The sled flips & I
tumble out, a bundle of pelts

trawled across frozen earth
until my numb fingers
let go. Quickly to my feet,

I galumph after, waist
deep in snow, barking
commands that my ancestors,

who spoke with all creatures, taught me,
but long gone, the yipping echoes
fade into nothingness. I stare

at the blank page, void
of direction, mine
an unwritten, unknown

history. No longer feeling
my legs, arms, anything, I fall.
When Karuka returns, hoary

coat clinging to her ribs, she licks
my face to wake me, I think,
before her fangs break my flesh.

THE HIGHFALUTIN OLD COOT

with the blue guitar lies unstrung
in the patient's chair, reflecting
that he hears things as they are, not
how they should be, the tired refrain
of his ancient fishwife blowing
her squawky mouth organ aboard
a southbound train, unchanging
              greenery scrolling by
like a Hanna-Barbera cartoon. Thing is,
he no longer has a wife because he chose not to
work at the fucking post office another
fucking second, sorting the sheer unknown
hell of standard business
                    envelopes & plain
brown wrappers. Things as they are,
he spits out, change with every strum &
twang of the transcendental
strings.
              O, poses one
haloed by fluorescent light, *what's wrong
with things you feel
         you must change them?*
The needle stings the graying blues man
as if a bee had bumbled into the flower
of his pried wide jaw. His gum tingles, his tongue
slowly numbs.
         Someday, Dr. Pappadopoulos pipes,
you'll learn to accept things as they are.
Pausing to tune his drill, he adds,
with a blackbird's cold stare: *Open up.*
A swell of instruments fills the old guitarist's
gaping pit. The dentist dives in,
                    whistling folksy
strains from *The Magic Flute.*

DEATHWHORE

When she swung her endless
gams into my spanking
         new baby
blue Infiniti coupe, Death
began making not
so subtle advances. Lengthy
lashes like swallows
fluttering across guileless
sky, she wanted me to pull off
onto the shoulder, among
daisies & thick honey-
         suckle, luring
laborious bees, but late
already, I knew I shouldn't, so
she kindly stooped
under the steering wheel & foot
to the gas, my lax
long fellow, doing zero
to boner in no time, slipped
past grazing teeth
         of unzipped
fly, past wet plump
parted lips–past the cherry
picker grinding
uphill. The short
stogie dangling from the scruffy wide-
         eyed Benzedrine driver's lip
dropped as I veered, hands at 10
         & 2, to merge
with downtown traffic. Velvety
head in my lap bobbing, I sped
through the changing
light at 8th & Eternity. A red-faced haus-
frau, church-sized
crucifix swinging from her rear-

view, nearly leaped out her unrolled minivan
window, fat brats strapped in back
          howling, horns
squawking, tires squelching & supercilious
sun kissing the glistening
helmet of the bronze
monument to the anonymous
multitudes who died for Truth
& Beauty because I couldn't, hips
heaving toward heaven,
stop. Nor could she, being
Death & knowing
every angle, swallow
my oeuvre raw.

THE GIRAFFE

wanders the night, head
lowered, lurking in sprawling
anonymity.
It glides along–long-legged, long-
faced–dips its neck & slips past

the forlorn monkey
bars & swing-less swing set. Up
the wooded hillock,
parked cars hump to "Yeah! Oh Yeah!"
A foot juts out an unrolled

glass, ankle bracelet
jangling. Flickering headlights
pass through dark, trembling
leaves. You can't see the giraffe
slumped behind a butterfly

bush, watching, listening
for the sake of national
security. For
you might be a terrorist.
We might all be terrorists.

WASHINGTON CROSSING THE DELAWARE

What does one pack
for a jaunt into history?
Honeywell reports: a change
of clothes, powder

for his periwig & a Fannie
Burney novel to pass
the night in Trenton. But for now, icy
clumps batter the klutzy

ferry. Frozen in his stance, boot
propped confidently atop
his duffel bag, he fixes
his determined gaze

upon New Jersey, drawing
closer as if
he willed it so, his ragged
troops slaving to propel

the Durham up-
stream, the turgid river
maintaining fierce
loyalty to the crown.

He stands, tattered
flag at his shoulder, saber
at his side, big hands
curled into fists.

Sudden Realization of the Perfect Thing to Have Said

On Washington crossing Delaware St.,
a vagrant hits me up for a cigarette.
Summer's peaking, yet he's wearing what smells like a pea
coat, caked with tobacco spit, Sterno,
Mad Dog 20/20 & other crud. I'm hip,
so I give him one–hell, I give him two–

but now he wants cash. What a plum tomato
from his fragrant perspective must exist
in my stead, sun shining like a chip
on the shoulder of my shirt, fresh from the launderette,
missing nary a button. So when I say no,
he snarls, wielding a salvaged skewer like an epee,

demands my wallet & says to make it snappy.
What to do–except try not to
snicker. Does he think I'm a Tippecanoe
billionaire-industrialist-turned-philanthropist
scoping out suitable locations for the proposed statuette
of me, waves of hair like licorice whips?

I'm a high school senior, hoping to land a scholarship,
I try to explain, but he's clearly not happy
to hear this. Perhaps he has a history with IVTC-Lafayette.
Perhaps years ago an apathetic instructor failed to
see the significance of one less dental hygienist
in the fold. How can anyone know

the effect he has on others? One domino
falls, then another, a causal relationship
forming with each plunk. The catalyst,
however, for human entropy
is often disguised, traveling incognito
throughout a lifetime, a faded silhouette

in a second-story window. Jabbing the attelet
into my baggy white chino
crotch, the bum snarls his face into
a red ball & having gained a bargaining chip,
swears if I don't fork it over, he'll lop off my pea-
shooter with the flick of his wrist.

Not wanting to sing falsetto, I empty my pocket.
The wino bolts down Delaware St., past the porno
shop & tattoo parlor. I yell after him, albeit ex post
facto, *I hope you blow the wad on aromatherapy!*

CAVEAT EMPTOR

Here he comes whistling up
the stoop, leaning
on the bell like the Reaper
himself, offering everything
from personalized
Good & Evil salt
& pep-
per shakers to Everlasting Light
bulbs if (ahem) the gentle-
man will allow
him a few
moments for a brief demon-
stration. O
the knot in the gut tightens
as the stranger, quirky
as his squeaky loafers, shiny
as shellac in his snake
skin suit, sidles in, but how
could a son of man not
succumb to the temptation of free
samples? *Now that's quality
you can feel*, touts
the salesman, extracting
a coil from his portmanteau
of discount, dis-
continued rope,
binding the prospective
buyer's arms & legs so
that his every orifice
is accessible, but all
for naught–he's long
sold. He wants
the lot, from the glow-
in-the-dark crowns
for his thorny grinning

grill to the Holy
        Stroller Land &
        Sea sandals
        with patented Miracle
        Sole technology. Days later,
        when the Great Chain
        of Bling on which he'd
        strung his gold-plated
        crucifix broke,
        he wept,
recalling the disclaimer
above.

is often beautiful. Sorrow,
spit from a fireplug uncorked
in a fatal pileup, drums
pity on black bumbershoots

opening like a Caillebotte
exhibit. Despondency
fills the cup of the young mother
slumped against a weathered

blue balustrade, checkered robe
undone & the colicky baby
sucking a melancholy breast,
having tasted despair too

early, grows up suicidal,
like Schumann, Van Gogh
or Marilyn Monroe maybe.
These days, seeing no one,

hearing nothing but moaning
& heavy breathing, climbing
the interminable flights
to my dark efficiency,

I sit beside the window, bare
elm branches straining
to hold a sky flushed
with artificial clouds. Dusk

palls mottled rooftops & just
when I think no hope is left,
the last dancing ray disappears
like Giselle into the forest.

ERATO & ERRATA

I contemplated runes, jabbed
                    pins into the desecrated
            temple of a voodoo doll. I tried abstinence,
    temperance, neither by choice. How-
ever much I prodded & poked
                    the remains of my brain, that inky
        day's portentous clouds mostly slunk by
                unnoticed as I was
                                looking up
        "precipitately" in my weathered
dictionary. Rain tapped the glass like the stiff
                keys of a Smith-
        Corona upon which the story began
                    to unravel along the common
                            thread dangling
        from the hem of a diaphanous blue
gown, revealing the inverted V of the lyrical
                legs of
        the Muse. *O Marty-poo!*
                she cooed, my dumbstruck
                        face lifting from the page. *You're so*
        cute–invoking your adolescent
notion of me, banging
                    out your novel
            stabs at poetry. There's no
                one like you anywhere–
                    & clever!
    What burst that gooey pink bubble–
another time perhaps. For all at once–out the window
                through which I threw the dead
            fern, fancy Greek urn & all, as she ran naked
                across the lawn with me
                            behind her shouting, *Fuck*
        you if I'm crazy–a fawn
stumbled from the brambles.

As in a dream,
I fell, a wet leaf stuck to the allusive
anvil, my chin tilted toward
whatever gods remained
sufficiently sober to supplicate. Where
could I turn, given the stars, given
her glower in every twinkle?

DORIS IN THE ALTOGETHER BY THE SEA

Against a coral backdrop,
anemones spiral out
of a wine carafe,
still life with fruit, while
in the foreground, a different
kind of peach, too pink,
too plump to be attractive,
Doris–unclothed &
unfamiliar with subtle
shades of elegance–shivers,
wearing but a string

of pearls, her flesh not
firm, but abundant.
Her hands, folded self-
consciously over
a patch of color,
light & fanciful
as Colette, at once
intimate & obfuscate
the curlicued waves of hair.
Every flowing curve

spills onto the bare wall. No
Monet, no Renoir, but framed
by open window,
nondescript
          houses
outline a beach shimmering
with shells, pagan deities,
desires, bright yellow
butterflies & swirling sun.

Deep in the forest
of masts, their sails in full bloom,

a rowboat splashes
through the speckled blue.
Oarsmen with bold, vigorous
strokes thrust the small craft,
a geometric
abstraction tilting
across the waves' mythic claws,
ever closer to the point
of unrecognizable

yet ordinary folks, backs
turned, fishing at the harbor.
Clouds swan toward the horizon,
dark as the robe draped
over the red oak
chair beside Doris,
whose breath & almost
aquarelle eyes reveal not
only ennui, but
also a foreboding storm.

As Wordsworth Wandered

He came upon the precipice & saw
the endless blue of sky & sea that reached
beyond & breathed the salty air of flaw-
less nature. *God's eternal extended*

finger to man, he scribbled, *given form*.
Not taken with that chapel ceiling's painting
of weary, vaguely Jove-like outstretched arm,
he found divinity in everything,

from some ten thousand dancing daffodils
beside the billowy, white-bearded waves
that kissed the jagged shore, to miles & miles
of woods unspoiled, disrobed of autumn leaves.

He also noted briefly as he fell
an odd cloud that looked like [illegible].

NEW SHOES

Not my diploma nailed to the wall, not
my wife, not my kids, not
that I know of, smiling, holding
hands at the roller rink. *Where's
my stuff?* I ask, sticking my big mug,
coffee steam trailing from
its lip, in every orifice–er, office–along
the long nightmare
of doors, behind which I find neither
tigers nor ladies, but blank,
indifferent shrugs. A hand grips
my shoulder:
*What seems to be
the problem?* It's Sheila. I share
my concerns about my position, as well
as my doubts about my fathering
the Kodak kids, which isn't meant
as a knock against the mother, for under
the right circumstances–
Listen, rocking
on her heels, Sheila interrupts, *since
you've never worked here, you're probably having
some kind of episode.* If I were strapped
to a hypnotic wheel, my head couldn't
have spun more.
     Is my face red? I blurt.
Don't worry about it, she says. *Rosacea's
treatable. Just try not to scratch.* Then calls
security. Elevator going
down, the box
of personal belongings I'm handed
on the way out casts suspicion on Sheila's
explanation, though, in her favor,
   I *do* itch. Suddenly blinded

by sunlight, I stumble over
a panhandler, spilling my life
scraps with his pencils
& change on the ratty blanket
that hides his amputated
legs. *Sorry*, I tell him, unsure
what I'm apologizing for–my clumsiness
or the cribbage pegs
he has for legs. He curses
& threatens, but I can't help
noting, with a surreptitious
snicker, that I got him by at least
two feet! Rising, I blow
a kiss to Sheila, who waves, for all
I know, from her glistering
window. It's just
like the old proverb about
the man with no shoes, except
I have shiny new loafers–
          so I kick him.

NOTES

In addition to appearances in print, "Hole" was featured as part of the "Not Somewhere Else But Here" episode of *Books Unbound*, a radio series produced by WFHB in Bloomington, Indiana. I wish to extend my appreciation to everyone at *Books Unbound*, especially to the readers for their exceptional presentation of the poem and to the series writer and producer, my great friend Cynthia Wolfe.

"Metaphysics of Baseball" spoofs Robert K. Adair's genuinely informative *The Physics of Baseball*.

As a song, "Walking in Chicago with a Suitcase in My Hand" utilizes a traditional blues motif, as in:

> *Walking in Chicago with a suitcase in my hand*
> *Yes, I'm walking in Chicago with a suitcase in my hand*
> *I got a ticket in my pocket, Prince Albert in a can*

Subsequent verses catalog various items that the singer purportedly has on his person, such as a quarter roll of Mentos, a "bad" penny depicting Lincoln facing both ways, a souvenir tongue depressor, the real lyrics to "Louie, Louie," pocket-lint-encrusted phenobarbital, *Quotations from Chairman Mao Tse-Tung*, assorted flatware and cutlery, and a greatly diminished pint of Beam. Although the poem may suggest otherwise, no known recording of Howlin' Wolf performing this song exists.

The title "The Distant Sea" comes from Rilke's *Letters to a Young Poet*, not the anime movie *Case Closed: Private Detective in the Distant Sea*.

The ideas and images for "Poem" draw upon various texts about surrealists and their work. Patrick Waldberg's *Surrealism* offers an in-depth overview of the movement's early days for anyone interested in those sorts of things.

The quotations in "On Looking Again at Boswell's Johnson" come not only from Boswell's famous biography, but from any number of other sources that provide quotations from Johnson and Boswell, including handwritten notes from a seminar I attended as a student.

"Spring Muzzle" was inspired by Georgette Heyer's *Sprig Muslin*.

While the painting described in "Doris in the Altogether by the Sea" belongs entirely to the realm of imagination, it resembles Dufy's *Amphitrite*. Indeed, much of the language for the poem owes to the depictions and analyses that Alfred Werner provides throughout his book *Raoul Dufy*.

HALF INCH PRESS